Baptism, Jesus, and Me

Baptism, Jesus, and Me

The Who, What, Why, When, and How of Your Baptism

Written by **David Butler**

Illustrated by **Ryan Jeppesen**

DESERET
BOOK

To Abby through Zach
and all you lovable crazies in between.
XO Your favorite uncle.
—D.B.

To my kids:
You amaze me every day. I hope you learn
from the truths found in this book. At the very least,
I hope you like the pretty pictures.
—R.J.

Text © 2016 David Butler
Illustrations © 2016 Ryan Jeppesen

Visit us at DeseretBook.com

Library of Congress Cataloging-in-Publication Data

Names: Butler, David, author. | Jeppesen, Ryan, illustrator.
Title: Baptism, Jesus, and me : the who, what, why, when, and how of baptism / David Butler ; illustrated by Ryan Jeppesen.
Description: Salt Lake City, Utah : Deseret Book, 2016. | Includes bibliographical references.
Identifiers: LCCN 2016020265 | ISBN 9781629722498 (paperbound)
Subjects: LCSH: Baptism—The Church of Jesus Christ of Latter-day Saints.
Classification: LCC BX8655.3 .B88 2016 | DDC 264/.09332081—dc23
LC record available at https://lccn.loc.gov/2016020265

Printed in China
RR Donnelley, Dongguan, China

10 9 8 7 6 5 4 3

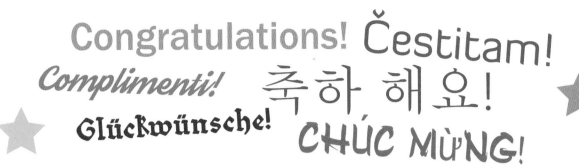

Congratulations! Čestitam! Complimenti! 축하 해요! Glückwünsche! CHÚC MỪNG!

Those are some ways people say *congratulations* in different places around the world. When someone gets baptized, that is a word that comes up a lot! The decision to be baptized is one of the most important DECISIONS you make in life. Your baptism day is a day that will change you forever.

Write the date you were baptized or will be baptized in this box.

> [ ]

Why is that day and decision so important?

This book will not only answer WHY, but also the WHO, WHAT, WHEN, and HOW of baptism!

This is a book you can read by yourself or with your family or someone who loves you. You will answer questions, do activities, and learn a lot about baptism, Jesus, and you! It might be fun to work on during Sunday afternoons or for family home evenings.

Get ready to discover and learn in a way that will help you both enjoy and remember your baptism day as one of the most important and happiest days of your life.

Congratulations!

Put a picture of you on your baptism day here.

Who?

Who is an important part of your baptism?
What part does each person play?

WHO is Heavenly Father?
WHO is Jesus Christ?
WHO is the Holy Ghost?
WHO are you?

WHO is Heavenly Father?

Heavenly Father is our Father and our God. When you are baptized, you make promises with Him. You lived with Him before you were born, and He sent you here for an important purpose. He has a plan for you to be happy, called the plan of salvation. Your Heavenly Father hears all of your prayers and knows all of your needs and wants.

Everything He does is to show love for you.

Activity: Heavenly Father sent you to this beautiful world to show you His love for you. Fill this box with some of Heavenly Father's creations. Cut out photos, draw pictures, or go out and collect some of His creations and tape them here.

Every time you see Heavenly Father's creations, you can remember that He made this beautiful world for you.

WHO is Jesus Christ?

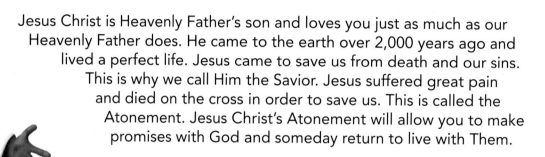

Jesus Christ is Heavenly Father's son and loves you just as much as our Heavenly Father does. He came to the earth over 2,000 years ago and lived a perfect life. Jesus came to save us from death and our sins. This is why we call Him the Savior. Jesus suffered great pain and died on the cross in order to save us. This is called the Atonement. Jesus Christ's Atonement will allow you to make promises with God and someday return to live with Them.

Jesus Christ makes Heavenly Father's plan of salvation possible for each one of His children.

Activity: This is a well-loved scripture from the Bible about Jesus Christ. Look up the scripture (or get some help looking it up) and fill in the blanks.

John 3:16

"For _____ so _____ the _____, that he gave his _____ _____ Son, that whosoever _____ in him should not _____, but have _____ _____."

Do you think you could memorize this verse?
Color in this star if you memorize it
and then recite it to someone.

WHO is the Holy Ghost?

The Holy Ghost is often called "the Spirit." Heavenly Father, Jesus Christ, and the Holy Ghost work together as a group called the Godhead. Their purpose is to love you, care for you, and help you become someone wonderful and great. The Holy Ghost has a special role as a messenger to confirm truth in your mind and heart and bring you the love and strength of Heavenly Father and Jesus Christ.

How do you recognize the Holy Ghost? Not everyone feels the Holy Ghost in the same way, but there are some common feelings people use to describe His influence.

Think about or try some of these experiences:

Sit close to a warm campfire or fireplace. Notice the feelings of warmth.

Wrap yourself up in a cozy blanket. Do you feel safe and secure?

Give someone you love a giant hug—make it last for at least ten seconds. Recognize how much love and protection you feel.

Stand in a dark room for a minute. Then turn on the light. How much more can you see with the light on?

Listen to a beautiful and sacred song with your eyes closed. Pay attention to the feeling of peace you have as you listen.

These activities might not give you the exact same feeling that the Holy Ghost does, but they can remind you of His peace, comfort, protection, and guidance. As you pay attention to your feelings, you can learn over time how the Holy Ghost communicates with and helps you.

WHO are you?

You are you!

You are a child of Heavenly Father, and you lived with Him as a spirit before you came to earth. When you were born, you left your heavenly home, and your spirit body entered into your little baby body. You might be small compared to the size of the world, but the spirit inside your body is MAGNIFICENT and INCREDIBLE! You lived for a long time before you were born, and you will continue to live forever. Forever!

You have remarkable potential, and God is helping you discover what that is.

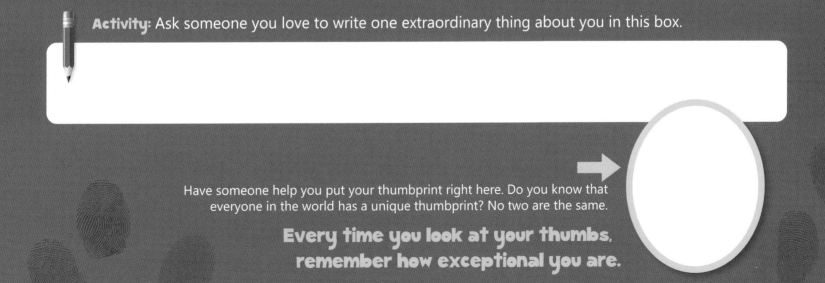

Activity: Ask someone you love to write one extraordinary thing about you in this box.

Have someone help you put your thumbprint right here. Do you know that everyone in the world has a unique thumbprint? No two are the same.

Every time you look at your thumbs, remember how exceptional you are.

More about WHO

You learned about **WHO** Heavenly Father is, **WHO** Jesus Christ is, **WHO** the Holy Ghost is, and **WHO** you are.

Here are some scriptures that you could read and study to learn more about the **WHO** of baptism. Some are about the Godhead, and some are about you. You might want to read them with someone who can explain more about what they mean.

John 3:16
Moses 1:39
Genesis 1:26–27
Mosiah 4:9–10
Doctrine and Covenants 8:2
Doctrine and Covenants 130:22–23
Articles of Faith 1:1

What?

Do you know what baptism is?
What is important to know about baptism?

WHAT is a covenant?
WHAT is an ordinance?
WHAT is baptism?
WHAT promises do you make at baptism?

Ask at least **FIVE** different people this question:

What is the first word that comes to your mind when you hear the word "baptism"?

Activity: Write all of their answers in this box. Use different sizes of letters and colors to create a collection of words about baptism.

There are many things people can say about baptism. **But WHAT is it?**

In order to understand what **BAPTISM** is, you must know what an **ORDINANCE** is.

In order to understand what an **ORDINANCE** is, you must know what a **COVENANT** is.

In order to understand what a **COVENANT** is, you must know what an **AGREEMENT** is.

Agreement ▸ **Covenant** ▸ Ordinance

WHAT is an AGREEMENT?

WHAT is a COVENANT?

There are many types of agreements.

Countries, businesses, and people all make agreements with each other. An agreement is a decision that two or more people make together. They make promises to each other and expect each other to keep their promises.

A COVENANT is a type of agreement. It is a sacred AGREEMENT between a person and the Lord.

When you enter a covenant, you make a promise with God, and He makes promises with you. He decides all of the promises of the covenant and then lets us choose if we want to accept it.

When you decide to make a **COVENANT**, you enter it, or show you agree, by participating in an **ORDINANCE**.

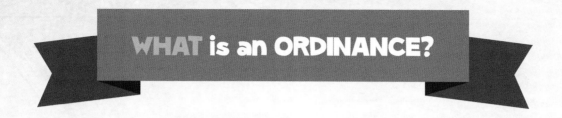

WHAT is an ORDINANCE?

Sometimes when we make promises with each other, we do some sort of action to show that we are making the promise. You might . . .

Lock pinkies in a pinky promise

Shake hands

Cross your heart

Sign a paper

The action is not the promise, but it is the sign that you agree to the promise. Heavenly Father has us participate in physical actions when we make promises with Him, too. These are called ORDINANCES.

An ORDINANCE is a sacred act or ceremony we perform to connect with God. ORDINANCES are necessary for us to make COVENANTS with God.

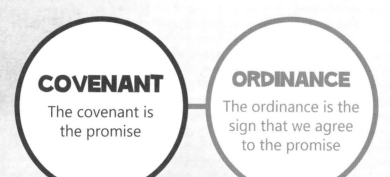

COVENANT
The covenant is the promise

ORDINANCE
The ordinance is the sign that we agree to the promise

All ordinances are performed by someone holding the **PRIESTHOOD**. The **PRIESTHOOD** is the power and authority (or permission) to act in the name of God.

So, WHAT is BAPTISM?

BAPTISM is an **ORDINANCE**. That means that **BAPTISM** is the ceremony you participate in to show you are making **COVENANTS** with God.

Two important ordinances are part of your baptism.

 The **FIRST** ordinance happens when a priesthood holder says a prayer and then lowers you into the water.

 The **SECOND** ordinance happens when a priesthood holder lays his hands on your head and says a blessing that bestows the gift of the Holy Ghost.

We will talk about these two parts in more detail later.

That was a lot! Let's review:

AGREEMENT	COVENANT	ORDINANCE
A decision between two people based on promises.	A sacred agreement between a person and the Lord.	A ceremony performed by a priesthood holder that shows you are agreeing to or entering a COVENANT.

BAPTISM: An ORDINANCE that we participate in to make certain COVENANTS with God. Remember, God has set the conditions and promises of this COVENANT, and we agree to accept and live them.

WHAT promises do you make at baptism?

Many of the promises of the baptism covenant are found in the Book of Mormon in **Mosiah 18:8-11**.

Activity: Highlight or underline the promises of the baptismal covenant found in Mosiah 18. Use one color for our promises to Heavenly Father, and use a different color for His promises to us.

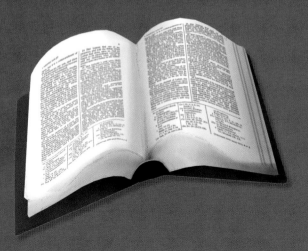

8 And it came to pass that he said unto them: Behold, here are the waters of Mormon (for thus were they called) and now, as ye are desirous to come into the fold of God, and to be called his people, and are willing to **bear** one another's **burdens**, that they may be light;

9 Yea, and are willing to **mourn** with those that **mourn**; yea, and **comfort** those that stand in

Bear: to help with

Burdens: hard things

Mourn: to be sad

Comfort: to make someone feel better

Stand as witness: represent and defend

Redeemed: saved

Eternal life: life with and like God

Abundantly: a lot

need of **comfort**, and to **stand as witnesses** of God at all times and in all things, and in all places that ye may be in, even until death, that ye may be **redeemed** of God, and be numbered with those of the first resurrection, that ye may have **eternal life**—

10 Now I say unto you, if this be the desire of your hearts, what have you against being baptized in the name of the Lord, as

a witness before him that ye have entered into a covenant with him, that ye will serve him and keep his commandments, that he may pour out his Spirit more **abundantly** upon you?

11 And now when the people had heard these words, they clapped their hands for joy, and exclaimed: This is the desire of our hearts.

Our promises to Him

The list on the left shows promises found in Mosiah 18 that we make with the Lord.
The list on the right shows different ways we can keep those promises.

Draw a line to match the promise on the left with the way we can keep it on the right.

Bear (help with) another's
burdens (hard things) ○

Mourn (be sad) with those
that mourn (are sad) ○

Comfort those that stand
in need of comfort ○

Stand as witnesses of
God at all times ○

Serve Him and others ○

Keep His commandments ○

○ Cheer up your brother when he
loses an important baseball game

○ Choose to be honest in
your schoolwork

○ Bear your testimony at church

○ Help your next-door neighbor
with a big yard project

○ Tell your friend you are sad
when his grandma dies

○ Carry your friend's backpack
when she is on crutches at school

Can you think of some other ways you can keep these promises?

His promises to us

When we are baptized, the Lord promises us some amazing things. Here are some of those promises:

You can be a member of His Church

You will be called His people

He will forgive you of your sins

You will receive eternal life

He will pour out His Spirit on you, and you will receive the gift of the Holy Ghost

More about WHAT

You learned about **COVENANTS, ORDINANCES**, and **BAPTISM**. You also learned about the promises of the baptismal covenant.

Here are some scriptures that you could read and study to learn more about the **WHAT** of baptism. You might want to read them with someone who can explain more about what they mean.

Mosiah 18:8–11
Doctrine and Covenants 20:77
John 3:1–5
Matthew 3:13–17
Bible Dictionary: Covenant
Bible Dictionary: Baptism

Why?

Everything Heavenly Father does has a reason.
Why is baptism so important?

WHY **did we come to earth?**
WHY **are we baptized?**
WHY **do we receive the gift of the Holy Ghost?**

Have you ever wondered **WHY** about some things?

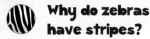 **Why do zebras have stripes?**　 **Why do so many dads snore?**　 **Why do wasps sting?**　 **Why do you have to do chores?**

 Activity: Write one of your own **WHY** questions here:

In order to understand WHY Heavenly Father asks us to get baptized,
we have to understand another WHY question first.

WHY did we come to earth?

Heavenly Father has a plan for us. He taught it to us before we were born. We wanted to be a part of it. This plan is often called the **PLAN OF SALVATION**. His plan was for us to come to earth to become more like Him. Here are three important purposes of His plan:

1. **We receive a body like His.**
2. **We form a family like His.**
3. **We learn to make choices to become perfect like Him.**

 Activity: Write some words or phrases that come to your mind when you think of Heavenly Father.

We lived with Heavenly Father before we came to this earth. In order for us to become more like Heavenly Father, we needed to leave His presence. **We want to return to Him** after we finish our purpose on earth.

Here on earth, there are two things that could keep us from becoming like Heavenly Father and living with Him again. Without the Savior's help, we could not overcome them.

Jacob, a prophet in the Book of Mormon, called the two things MONSTERS because of how scary they would be if we faced them alone (see 2 Nephi 9:10, 19, 26).

Their names are

DEATH and **SIN**.

DEATH keeps us separated from our bodies and separated from God's home. We do not have the power to return by ourselves.

SIN is any action that goes against God's commandments. Sin makes us weak, unclean, and unable to live with God. Sin is impossible to get away from by ourselves.

These monsters might seem scary because they could keep us away from our Heavenly Father and eternal life.

But here is the GOOD NEWS . . .

The GOOD NEWS is Jesus Christ!

Both of these "monsters" would be scary if we faced them on our own. The **GOOD NEWS** is you don't have to! **You have a SAVIOR! A HERO!**

That hero is Jesus Christ!

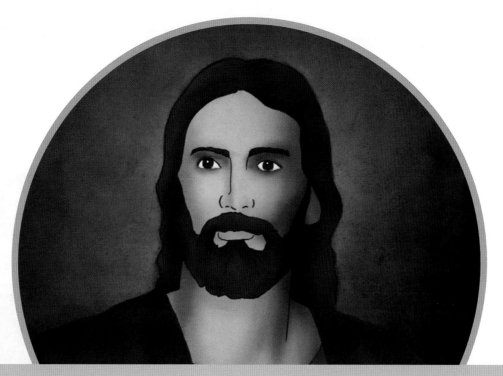

Jesus Christ came to earth and defeated the monsters of DEATH and SIN. Because of Jesus Christ, we can return to live with Heavenly Father and those we love. We can enjoy eternal life. This is why we call Him our Savior.
The plan of salvation only works because of the Savior Jesus Christ.

Prophets and angels have been spreading this **GOOD NEWS** since the beginning of the world. The word **GOSPEL** means **GOOD NEWS**.

"O how great the goodness of our God, who prepareth a way for our escape from the grasp of this awful monster. . . . O the greatness of the mercy of our God, the Holy One of Israel!"

2 Nephi 9:10, 19

JESUS CHRIST saved us from death and sin through His Atonement. The Atonement of Jesus Christ took place when He suffered in the Garden of Gethsemane and died for us on the cross.

The **RESURRECTION** of Jesus Christ guarantees that everyone will overcome death, be resurrected, and return to the presence of Heavenly Father.

Jesus Christ also offers to us the gift of **FORGIVENESS** from our sins. He offers us a chance to become clean again. This is a gift we first choose to accept when we are baptized and continually choose through repentance.

This picture shows an example of the path to return to Heavenly Father and become like Him.

Activity: Draw a bridge over the first pit to represent what Jesus Christ did to overcome death.

When Jesus died and was resurrected, the first "bridge" was built. The "monster" of death cannot hold us back. This is God's gift to all people, whether they have been baptized or not.

Covenant Path

Gate of Baptism

Death

BAPTISM is the gate to the path to eternal life. This covenant path is a gift from God that we must choose to accept. Being baptized shows that we accept Jesus Christ's help and His gift of eternal life.

Activity: Draw a long path leading from the gate all the way to eternal life.

When Jesus Christ suffered and died for our sins, the second bridge was built. It provided a way to overcome our sins. Jesus Christ is the only way to eternal life.

Eternal **Life**

Sin

Activity: Draw ladders leading from the pit of sin back up to the path.

After baptism, we will still make mistakes. When we sin, we fall off of the path. The Atonement of Christ allows us to repent and climb back up to the path. The fall will hurt, but Jesus Christ helps us escape the monster of sin, be forgiven, and continue on our journey.

WHY do we receive the gift of the Holy Ghost?

Do you remember the ordinance after baptism we mentioned earlier? This ordinance is called confirmation. During your confirmation, you receive the gift of the Holy Ghost.

What is the best gift you have ever received?

The gift of the Holy Ghost is the **GREATEST** gift Heavenly Father gives us while we are on this earth.

When you are confirmed, you receive this gift. You can then receive the Holy Ghost's help throughout your whole life!

The Gift of the Holy Ghost

Gives us the constant companionship of a member of the Godhead

Brings us strength to do hard things

Comforts us in times of trouble and sadness

Helps us make choices that will bring us closer to God

Helps us avoid future sin

The gift of the Holy Ghost will help you become like Heavenly Father and return to Him someday. Look inside this gift, which represents the gift of the Holy Ghost, to see some of the reasons why this gift is so **WONDERFUL**.

Temple

Eternal **Life**

Baptism is the gate to enter the covenant path. This same path also passes through the temple. In the temple, we make more **COVENANTS** and are given more **GIFTS** to help us on our journey. All of these gifts from our Heavenly Father help us become more like Him and return to Him someday.

Activity: Ask some of your older family members this question and write or draw their answers along the path.

"What other blessings has Heavenly Father given us to help us on the path?"

Examples: scriptures, families, and so on.

More about WHY

We learned **WHY** we came to this earth and why we need the help of **JESUS CHRIST**. We also learned why we are baptized and receive the **GIFT OF THE HOLY GHOST**.

Here are some scriptures that you could read and study to learn more about the **WHY** of baptism. You might want to read them with someone who can explain more about what they mean.

2 Nephi 9:1–26
2 Nephi 31 (the WHOLE chapter!)
2 Nephi 32:1–3
John 3:1–17
Bible Dictionary: Holy Ghost

When?

WHEN can a person be baptized?

WHEN is a person ready to make that choice?

Will anyone miss the chance to be baptized?

WHEN can a person be baptized?

People can be baptized at almost any age. Some people are baptized when they are 8, 15, 45, or 99. They can be baptized whenever they are ready. **Heavenly Father has taught us that the earliest He wants us to be baptized is EIGHT years old.**

Activity: Try building a sand castle or a block tower with a younger sibling or friend.

Who built a stronger castle or tower? Why?

What other things can you do better now than when you were younger?

Here are two of the reasons why Heavenly Father has asked us to wait until we are eight to be baptized:

1. When we are baptized, we make important promises to follow Jesus Christ. Someone who is eight is old enough to understand and keep the promises he or she makes.

2. Before we are eight years old, we cannot sin. (Remember the monster of sin?) Sin has no power over people before they are eight, which means they don't need baptism.

There are many people in this world who do not know about Jesus Christ, baptism, or covenants when they are EIGHT years old.

Heavenly Father sends missionaries all over the world to teach people about the gospel of Jesus Christ and invite them to be baptized. They are always looking for people to teach about the Savior.

You can be a missionary too! As you live as a witness of Jesus Christ in your words and example, you help other people come closer to Him and learn more about Him.

Activity: If someone asked you why Jesus Christ is so special and important to you, what would you say?

Will anyone miss the chance to be baptized?

EVERYONE will have a chance to accept Jesus Christ and be baptized. Even people who have died. When we die, our spirit goes to a place called the spirit world. We wait there until the Resurrection.

People in the spirit world can learn, change, and choose to accept Jesus Christ. However, they do not have bodies and so they cannot be baptized themselves.

Heavenly Father is kind and has allowed people who are still on earth (and who have bodies) to be baptized for people who have died. **We call this baptism for the dead.** These baptisms are done inside temples.

Activity: When you are twelve, you can go to the temple and be baptized for your ancestors. Have someone show you how you can get on the computer and find the names of people in your family who died without a chance to be baptized. This is called family history work.

Color in one of these people when you help find the name of a person for whom baptism can be done in the temple.

AFTER Baptism

Have you ever forgotten anything? Someone's name? Your lunch? To clean your room?

It is very easy to forget. One thing we do not ever want to forget is Jesus Christ and the promises we have made with Him and Heavenly Father.

This is one of the reasons Heavenly Father has given us the ordinance of the sacrament.

During the sacrament, we eat bread and drink water to witness (or promise) to Heavenly Father that we will **remember the Savior** and our promises. We also think about the times we have not kept our covenants, and we make promises to do better.

We are baptized and receive the gift of the Holy Ghost only once in our life, but we participate in the ordinance of the **sacrament** every Sunday at church to help us remember our promises and continue progressing on the covenant path.

Activity: The sacrament is a very sacred time to remember Jesus Christ and what He has done for us. What is something you can do before and during the sacrament to help make it a meaningful experience?

More about WHEN

You learned about WHEN people are baptized. You also learned more about those who did not have a chance to get baptized on the earth and WHEN you can start helping them.

Here are some scriptures that you could read and study to learn more about the WHEN of baptism. You might want to read them with someone who can explain more about what they mean.

Moroni 8:8–12
Doctrine and Covenants 68:25, 27
Doctrine and Covenants 128:12–18
1 Corinthians 15:29

How?

HOW do we know who can perform baptisms?

HOW does Heavenly Father want us to be baptized?

HOW do we know who can perform baptisms?

 Activity: Look at a map with someone and figure out how far **70 miles** is.

How long do you think it would take to walk that far?

This is a map of the place where Jesus lived while He was on the earth.

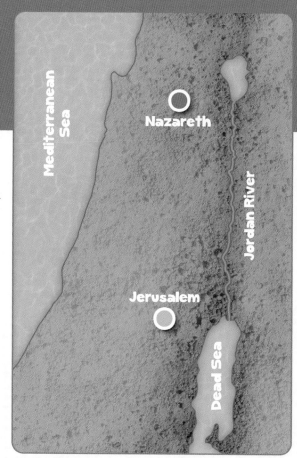

Jesus lived in Nazareth and went all the way to the Jordan River near Jerusalem to be baptized. **THAT WAS ABOUT 70 MILES AWAY!** Why would He do that?

He went to find a man named **JOHN THE BAPTIST**. John the Baptist was a man who had permission from Heavenly Father to baptize Jesus. He held the priesthood.

Priesthood authority is the permission to act or perform an ordinance in Heavenly Father's name.

Activity: Who baptized (or will baptize) you? Write his name here: ⟶

Ask that person if he has his **PRIESTHOOD LINE OF AUTHORITY**. A line of authority is a chart that traces a person's priesthood authority all the way back to Jesus Christ. Fill in this blank chart with the names from the line of authority of the person who baptized or will baptize you.

The person who baptized you (or will baptize you) has the priesthood, or the authority or permission from Heavenly Father to perform ordinances.

JESUS CHRIST

HOW does Heavenly Father want us to be baptized?

Not only was Jesus baptized with the same authority as you will be (or were), but He was baptized in the same way as you.

Do you know what a symbol is? A symbol is a number, color, object, or action that represents or makes you think about something else. For example, a lion can represent courage, or the color yellow can represent happiness. A thumbs-up action can represent, "Good job!"

We learn more about Jesus and about ourselves through the symbols of baptism.

When we are baptized, we dress in white clothes and go into a font or other body of water. A person with the priesthood says the baptismal prayer and then puts us completely under the water and pulls us back up again.

Here are the symbols we will talk about.

What do you think they teach?

White clothing

The water

Immersion (completely under the water)

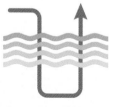

The motion of going down and coming up

The font or body of water

	What it teaches about YOU	What it teaches about JESUS
White clothing: White symbolizes purity and cleanliness.	You are making a decision to allow Jesus Christ to cleanse you from sin throughout your life.	Jesus Christ was the only person on earth who was perfectly clean and pure. He never committed a sin.
Water: Water symbolizes cleanliness. It also symbolizes the water in a mom's womb when she is having a baby.	Baptism is the start of a new life, just like when a baby starts life by being born.	Jesus called Himself the Living Water. We cannot live without water, and we cannot live without Jesus.
Immersion: Immersion means you go completely under the water.	Your decision to be baptized will completely change your life. It also shows that you want Jesus to be a part of your whole life.	Jesus gave His whole, complete life to Heavenly Father.
Going down and then back up: This symbolizes death and resurrection.	It is a symbol that you will put your old life down and then come up to start a new one as a follower of Jesus Christ.	Jesus Christ's death and Resurrection allow you to benefit from your baptism.
The font or body of water: This symbolizes both a grave and a mom's womb.	It is a perfect place for the death of our old life and the birth of our new life.	Jesus went below all things in His sacrifice for us. He died so we could live. He allows us to be "born again."

Jesus Christ told a man named Nicodemus that a person must be born again in order to enter heaven. This means that a person must live a new kind of life—**A LIFE LIKE JESUS.** When we are baptized, we bury our old life and promise to start a new one. The only reason we can start again is because of Jesus.

After we are baptized, we are confirmed and receive the gift of the Holy Ghost.

The person who was baptized sits in a chair while priesthood holders stand in a circle, place their hands on the person's head, and give a special ordinance blessing.

The circle: Circles symbolize protection. We are protected through our covenants and priesthood power.

A circle also represents eternity. It has no beginning or end.

The priesthood holder: In baptism and confirmation, the priesthood holder represents the Lord. He speaks for and in behalf of Him.

The hands on the head: Hands are placed on a head to symbolize the transfer of something from one person to another. In a blessing ordinance, hands are touching your head to symbolize power and gifts being given to you from Heavenly Father.

"Receive the Holy Ghost": These are some of the first words we hear in the confirmation ordinance. This is an invitation to the person receiving the blessing to live in a way to always have His Spirit.

More about HOW

We learned about **HOW** priesthood authority is important, **HOW** a person is baptized, and the meaning of baptismal symbols.

Here are some scriptures that you could read and study to learn more about the HOW of baptism. You might want to read them with someone who can explain more about what they mean.

Mark 9:4–10

Bible Dictionary: Baptism

3 Nephi 11:22–28

Romans 6:3–10

Doctrine and Covenants 84:27–28

Doctrine and Covenants 13

Can you remember the most beautiful place you have ever seen? Some places are beautiful to the eyes. Other places are beautiful to the heart. Read Mosiah 18:30 and see why the place called the Waters of Mormon was beautiful to the people there.

As life goes on, your baptism day will become more and more beautiful to you. You will remember it as the day you decided to follow your Savior, Jesus Christ.

When Alma taught the people who were gathered at the Waters of Mormon about baptism,

They clapped their hands for joy.

(Mosiah 18:11)

The more you learn about your baptism, the more it will make you want to clap your hands for joy and gratitude for Heavenly Father and Jesus Christ.

Congratulations on your decision to be baptized!